**Items should be returned to any Gloucestershire County Library on or before the date stamped below. This book remains the property of the Brockworth Community Library and can be renewed in person or by telephone by calling 01452 862 730**

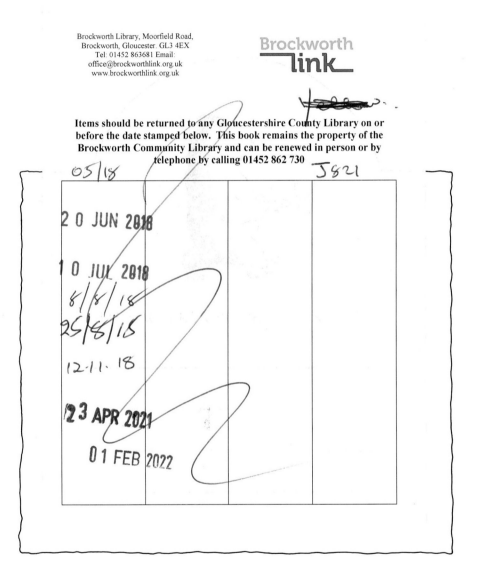

05/18          J821

2 0 JUN 2018

1 0 JUL 2018

8/8/18

25/8/18

12·11·18

23 APR 2021

0 1 FEB 2022

To Chris –
for making dreams come true
J. H.

For Helen with love
M. B.

First published 1998
by Walker Books Ltd
87 Vauxhall Walk
London SE11 5HJ

This edition published 1999

10 9 8 7 6 5 4 3 2

Text © 1998 Judy Hindley
Illustrations © 1998 Mike Bostock

This book has been typeset in Weiss.

Printed in Hong Kong

British Library Cataloguing
in Publication Data
A catalogue record for this book is
available from the British Library.

ISBN 0-7445-6332-1

# A SONG of COLOURS

Judy Hindley

illustrated by
Mike Bostock

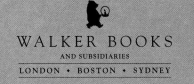

WALKER BOOKS
AND SUBSIDIARIES
LONDON · BOSTON · SYDNEY

# BLUE

Blue of distance, blue of sloes,

willow pattern, men in woad;

bright-sky-blue, electric-blue,

delphinium- and dolphin-blue,

giant-stairs-of-water-blue

where the sea steps down

from the shore.

Azure, aqua, indigo,

shadows in the purest snow,

midnight, peacock, royal blue,

true blue, goblin-blue;

blue in the glinty flares of ice,

splintery crystal-blue of eyes,

hot quick blue of a dragonfly;

blur of blue

that bites through a match

where it burns to a crooked black.

Ice-blue, blue of dusk,

robin's egg, forget-me-not;

blue of the bubble of Earth in space,

looking back from the moon.

# RED

Shimmering throat
of hummingbird –
a stab, a flash, a splash of it!
Poppies, cherries, roses, bricks,
rubies, blood and traffic lights.
Studded, clustered berries bright
on wreaths and vines
and autumn hedges;
bunting, flags and
lipstick kisses;
jewelled glow of rabbit's eyes.
Solemn dark of crimson room,
angry spark of ancient star,
staccato march of palace guard;
length of scarlet path unrolled
for kings
and princesses
and brides.

# WHITE

White of paper,

milk, and snow,

ermine trim on royal robes;

white of giant bears and owls,

clouds and daisies, chalk and horn,

a shining castle, sun-bleached bone.

White of gulls that flash and turn

and dip and scatter round the sky.

White of foam. The whites of eyes.

White of ghosts and teeth and stones

and ivory and angel robes;

white of a face when it's ill,

or old, and crinkled as paper.

White that's cold.

White of the smooth inside of an egg.

Froth of white on a birthday cake!

White of moonlight, blue and still,

of seashells, feathers,

pillows,

pearls.

# YELLOW

Spice and starfish,
fire and bees,
duckling-colour,
blackbird's beak;
dandelions, butter, gold,
soft-coloured stone
when the sun is low.
Poisonous film
on chemical pools:
milky, cloudy, mineral ooze.
Turning trees and ripening fields,
a butterfly, a Guernsey cow;
a shimmering palomino horse.
Most of Egypt, sandy-vast;
yolks, lemons, corn, brass…
The hair of girls in fairytales,
spinning straw to gold.

# PINK

Pink that's shocking,

loud as a shout,

like tropical fish

with fins that furl and flare

outrageously as wings!

Flamingo feathers, coral reefs;

a swollen sun in a sea of cloud

when all the sky is a blaze of pink.

Pink that startles, raw as a prawn;

a sunburned neck, a neon sign;

pink that gleams its tiny lights

in a smear of oil,

in suds, in bubbles.

Pink that's sugary.

Pink that's sweet.

Strawberry ice-cream. Fingernails.

Babies' fingers, soles of feet;

the quiet pink,

sometimes,

of dawn –

the huge inside

of a hippo's yawn.

# ORANGE

What a comical, cheerful thing it is

in marigolds,

and marmalade,

and gingery, carroty hair –

a toucan's beak,

an occasional cat,

a pumpkin plot,

an apricot.

Then it erupts like Vesuvius,

awesome as tiger fur!

# GREY

Is it dim, or is it bright?

Moss, mouse, rabbit-soft,

mushroom, fawn and fog,

or silvery slate of leafless trees,

shingle beaches,

roofs and walls?

Does it swim with rainbow lights?

Is it nearly pearly white?

Does it shimmer, does it gleam,

does it glisten, does it glint?

Quartz, opal, pewter, smoke.

A spoon,

a knife,

a rainy dawn.

# BROWN

Umber,

amber,

ochre, tan;

honey-gold brick

of a mud-built town;

topaz and mahogany;

sienna, sepia and sand.

Milky chocolate, dun and snuff;

cobnuts bursting from their pelts;

chestnut, sorrel, roan and bay;

toffee, coffee, butterscotch.

# BLACK

Black of liquorice, black of print,

black of charcoal, black of soot;

twisted black of a candlewick.

Panther-black. Black of a crow.

Black of the sky

on a moonless midnight

(polished and bedecked with stars).

Black of the dark

in caves and furrows,

pits and rifts and clefts and holes.

Bat- and ant- and beetle-black.

Fresh-laid tarmac, soft and hot.

Highways glistening with rain.

Pitch. Tar.

Iron. Ink.

Jet. Coal. Angus bull.

Black of the loam beneath the gold

where the plough cuts through

the stubble corn –

ebony rooster on a roof,

with a scarlet comb, in the snow.

# GREEN

Apple-green

and acid-green

and olive green

and pea.

Leafy,

grassy,

emerald:

wave, leaf, sea.

Tiny, curly lichen;

moss green,

lawn.

Jade, lime,

bottle-green.

Lizard in a weedy pond.

# PURPLE

The dark of shadows next to green,

arabesques in a weedy stream;

glossy as plum or aubergine;

dim of the clefts

in the twists of a tree;

or scars of mud

on a low, green hill

bitten with burrows

of rabbits or moles.

The pale-grey glimmering mist of it

in the blur of hundreds

of leafless twigs

where catkins hang their gold.

Mauve, lilac, amethyst;

crocuses, orchids, irises;

maroon, magenta, fuchsia, grape.

The hush of velvet robes.

# MANY-COLOURED

Many colours, any colours,

splattering in stars:

rocket-bursting multiple explosions

in the dark.

Gleaming buttons in a jar,

glistening like sweets.

Polka-dots and sugar-drops,

strips and stripes and beads,

and palettes, and kaleidoscopes,

and Joseph's many-coloured coat!

Multi-coloured ribbons streaming

all around a pole,

misty, airy bands of colour melting in a bow.

Paisley-pattern butterfly,

peacock-feather shawl,

prisms casting crystal fires

that dance along a wall...

Swirling from the blackness,

whirling into white,

spinning on a colour wheel –

dissolving

into light.

# MORE WALKER PAPERBACKS
## For You to Enjoy

Some more non-fiction rhyming texts

### THINK OF AN EEL
by Karen Wallace/Mike Bostock

Winner of the Times Educational Supplement's Junior Information Book Award and the Kurt Maschler Award

Can there be any creature as mysterious or magical as an eel? Born far away in the
Sargasso Sea, eels swim for thousands of miles to the very same river in which their parents lived.
Join one on this amazing journey.

"Simply stunning… An extraordinarily impressive book… Beautifully written …
superb illustrations." *Children's Books of the Year*

0-7445-3639-1   £4.99

### THE WHEELING AND WHIRLING-AROUND BOOK
by Judy Hindley/Margaret Chamberlain

This book is filled with the wonder of things that spin and whirl, that wheel and reel and roll,
that curve and coil and curl – pizzas, planets, sausage dogs,
bike springs, ice-cream cones, helter skelter rides…

"Reads like a Catherine wheel. The words sparkle with vitality, while Margaret Chamberlain's pictures dazzle…
Unusual and informative." *Junior Education*

0-7445-4730-X   £4.99

### A PIECE OF STRING IS A WONDERFUL THING
by Judy Hindley/Margaret Chamberlain

Have you ever thought about string and what an amazing thing it is? How do you suppose people
managed without it? And how on earth did they think it up? This book unravels the mystery!

"A thoroughly stimulating read." *The Sunday Telegraph*

0-7445-3637-5   £4.99

Walker Paperbacks are available from most booksellers, or by post from B.B.C.S., P.O. Box 941, Hull, North Humberside HU1 3YQ

24 hour telephone credit card line 01482 224626

To order, send: Title, author, ISBN number and price for each book ordered, your full name and address,
cheque or postal order payable to BBCS for the total amount and allow the following for postage and packing:
UK and BFPO: £1.00 for the first book, and 50p for each additional book to a maximum of £3.50.
Overseas and Eire: £2.00 for the first book, £1.00 for the second and 50p for each additional book.

Prices and availability are subject to change without notice.